By Joel Oppenheimer

Poetry
Four Poems to Spring (1951)
The Dancer (1951)
The Dutiful Son (1956)
The Love Bit and Other Poems (1962)
Sirventes on a Sad Occurrence (1969)
In Time: Poems 1962-1968 (1969)
On Occasion: Some Births, Deaths, Weddings,
     Birthdays, Holidays and Other Events (1973)
The Woman Poems (1975)
Acts (1976)
Names, Dates and Places (1978)
Houses (1980)
Just Friends/Friends & Lovers (1981)
At Fifty (1982)
Del Quien Lo Tomo (1983)
The Ghost Lover (1983)
Notes Toward a Definition of David (1984)
New Spaces: Poems 1975-1983 (1985)

Drama
The Great American Desert (1966)

Fiction
Pan's Eyes (1974)

Non-Fiction
The Wrong Season (1973)
Marilyn Lives (1981)
Poetry, the Ecology of the Soul (1983)

JOEL OPPENHEIMER

NEW SPACES

POEMS 1975-1983

BLACK SPARROW PRESS
SANTA BARBARA --- 1985

NEW SPACES: POEMS 1975-1983. Copyright © 1985 by Joel Oppenheimer.
All rights reserved. Printed in the United States of America. No part of
this book may be used or reproduced in any manner whatsoever without
written permission from the publisher except in the case of brief quota-
tions embodied in critical articles and reviews. For information address
Black Sparrow Press, P.O. Box 3993, Santa Barbara, CA 93130.

Some of these poems have appeared (in earlier versions) in *St. Andrews
Review, White Pine Journal, # Magazine, Credences, The Chicago Review,
The New York Times Sunday Magazine, The Perishable Press.*

Library of Congress Cataloging in Publication Data
Oppenheimer, Joel.
    New spaces.

    I. Title.
PS3529.P69N4   1985   811'.54   85-9060
ISBN 0-87685-641-5
ISBN 0-87685-640-7 (pbk.)
ISBN 0-87685-642-3 (signed ed.)

Table of Contents

New Spaces: Poems 1975—1983

The book is for the friends who have
stood by me in the new spaces.

Drawing from Life

STATEMENT TO THE CITIZENS

we are here, working,
hungering for bread.

you are there, living,
hungering.

        can there not
be commerce between us

THESE DAYS

all the young mothers
used to say
they didn't mind
the kids in the park
it was the other mommas
they had to talk to
being stuck there

the fathers said
they didn't mind
that so much
it was the kids

now i see the
bank street park
is filled with
poppas watching
babies crawl

the mommas stand
to the side talking

neither doing
what it wants
and maybe not
the babies either

TALKING

all of us
sit together
in the bar

some of us
are drinking

all of us
see the ghosts
before us

some of us
talk with them
and the rest
run to each other

we are talking
about him
whether with each other
or the ghosts

we are talking
about him
where he lies
alone on a bed
with ghosts
too alive
to bear

and there are always
more than enough
ghosts to talk to

all those voices
we carry within

those voices
that eat us up

lying alone on that bed
ghosts visit him

what they say
may be important
but we have to come out
come out of ourselves

there are conversations
with real people
waiting for us

CAMILLE OLDER

everything i have learned
is scratched into me
deeply as can be

i cough this morning
getting up
and it is 1951

where did dan go

why aren't we laughing

comparing the rasp
of our morning barks

why is this cough different

scaring me
heart into mouth

thinking of mother death
and her house

thinking of waking alone there
without friends

NATHANIEL'S VALENTINE

very beautiful picture for
my mom
                    it is broken after *beau,*
ful, picture, and *my.*   the m
in *my* is a w.   opposite on a
blue field the figure sits.
the part below the waterline a
fish a boat?   above facelike perhaps
a man.   straight lines as in
buildings, the building we
live in.   is this my son
forming?   jung might say so.
the lettering runs on brown, the
two sheets neatly pasted together

to form a page in this book.

THE ANSWER NOT GIVEN

you worry about which clothes
to cover you in which situation

what is it i'm not allowed
to objectify having found
you beautiful all ways

the clothes or fit were not
what prompted the response

i cannot of course deny
that they gave me pleasure

yet you have presented yourself
as object to all the others
and i have responded differently
from the very beginning

i found you beautiful i've said
but then i did not understand

ONE DAY AT A TIME

he said that thursday said
it would be friday's friend

he said this because he was waiting
because on friday he would get
a belated christmas gift
and he had asked me
when friday would get here

i said it would get here
right after thursday

hooray for thursday he said
he said that thursday said
he would be friday's friend

i wish i could be that clear-headed
that relaxed about waiting

like being able to say
that the night before the night
we finally touch each other
is that night's friend

THIS WAS SOME SORT OF HAIKU

we lived together ten years
and i curled my fingers
in your brown hair
brushed it
even washed it for you

we meet in the park
you tell me smiling
not to laugh at you
but i notice nothing

one hour later
my new friend, curly-haired,
laughing while she does so
tells me about your haircut
tells me how strange it looks

THE MODERNIST

he said
study greek
and latin
if you want
to be a poet

he said
only the sounds
matter not
the meaning

those were the
first two lessons

then he stopped
coming to class

LEGEND

a cairn is
a marker of rocks
thrown up over
the hero's grave

or points the way

end or beginning
or both still
thing placed by path

not to know
what it stands for
since the knowing
just might stop us

to know only
that it stands
points down or out
and that we ought
to do something

i have erected
this cairn but
do not know yet
if i am buried here
or have moved on

leaving this sign
for who comes next

there may be
another ahead

NIGHT AND DAY

the man in the
picture looks down
from the wall over
the bed lent for
the night
        for tom
he says *who gives*
beauty fully

i fall asleep in
that elegance of
phrase thinking how
i am always at
a loss when asked
for an inscription

i will steal this
to use as my
own
      certainly
also i must think

to give photographs
instead of books

in the morning i
look again
        it says

to tom who drives
beautifully
            i am
relieved
            but will
send the photo
anyway
            inscribed

NINE TO FIVE

still they ask for poems
as blessing on their union
and we give them

unconvinced of efficacy
in fact discouraged
but they are not

they ask for poems
we give them

hoping hoping this time
it will flourish
despite the poem

the wonder is
we keep writing
they keep getting married
life goes on

GRANT US

the story of a forty-
three going on forty-
four year old man and
a just turned thirty-
one year old woman and
what they did not
know about themselves
or the world and what
they thought they might
find out if they could
make it through one way
or another is the title
of the novel in progress

it will take a great
deal of money if not
time and also effort

THE ROCK AND THE HARD PLACE

not the gull
picking the bone.
not the trees.
not the fog
rolling in.

no part of me
yet. i am
watching and
listening. i
am loosening.

no right to
respond. no
right to respond.
i don't know
these things
by heart.

the lessons
come hard, friend
keeping your
mouth shut unless
you know. not
to take in the
new places too
quickly, not
to write what
you don't know.

WAKING IN BED BY A RINGING TELEPHONE

Whose call this is I think I know.
Her voice is in Toronto, though;
She does not see me lying here
Naked, with a need to go.

Her little ears must think it queer
To hear me cough and wheeze so clear
As lungs wake up and rattles shake
The nicest waking of the year.

She gives my ears, for my self's sake,
The sense that this is no mistake.
The outer sounds I have to leap
Are starting trucks and screeching brake.

Her words are lovely, dark and deep,
So we have promises to keep,
And miles to go before we sleep,
And miles to go before we sleep.

DOING IT

isn't it beautiful
the act of printing

action of ink on type on paper

the fiber gives gently when
just kissed so the ink flows in

the poem acts spread out on paper

the letter says 'the god awful winds
knocked over & pulled up over
a hundred huge & lovely oaks so
i have been cleaning all this up
made a brush pile of dead branches
easy to break off came back
& proofed the poem acts'

reading the letter and
seeing the proof enclosed
knowing the catbox is waiting
to be cleaned i do it
                    i do this
shit isn't it beautiful
we go on doing both
we clean up
            we do this

LIFE STUDIES

the outer surface of
the thigh
when flexed
shows a groove
longitudinally
which corresponds to
the ilio-tibial band

the stroking of
the inner interior
aspect of the upper
thigh of a woman
leads to geigl's reflex
in poupart's ligament

in men this is known
as the cremasteric reflex

i learned all this
as we stood in the bookstore
watching women ride bicycles
up the slight incline
of the street outside
from my friend the owner
who translates medical texts
and thus has much to teach

i saw that the women's
breasts turned into dugs

as they leaned over
the handlebars so
i was reminded of
mother wolf her
dugs hanging down to
feed the hungry twins
romulus and remus
before they built us rome

our other friend is much
more primitive and hopelessly
obsessed with muscles
of the ass which ball themselves
to fight the uphill grade

he contents himself
with such lascivious thoughts

this was a pleasant
afternoon entertainment

the next day i slept through
that bright sun and was
awakened harshly by linguistics

a neighbor screamed :
please come in!
come back in goddamnit!
please come back *in*!
don't be a fucking cunt asshole!
for god's sake come back into the house!
i don't care how many rags you got on!
please come in!
i want to talk to you . . .

she had been sitting
in the car warming it up

the motor slowed and stopped
the cardoor opened and slammed
the housedoor opened and slammed
they were both inside

i was awake
                and startled

no longer watching
safe with friends
learning
          i had been
enlisted in
a private war

and for that whole month
their car stayed parked
and i never once saw them

and the girls on bicycles
kept going up the hill
and we kept watching
from the bookstore

A LATE WINTER POEM

dying a slow death
dying small deaths
dying by pieces

what shall we tell

piece by piece

we who adjust
we who move on
we who move out
of the sun when
it burns us   we
who move into
the sun when we're
cold   we who know
enough to come in
out of the rain

we who adjust and
keep on living
and feel vaguely
less because of it

oh we who have
it all knocked up
because we give
inch by grudging
inch and keep on
living   we who live.

FOR DANIELLE

although gesell would say
doesn't he always
she's far too young
isn't she always
i kept thinking
how williams saw and wrote

A CHINESE TOY

Six whittled chickens
on a wooden bat

that peck within a
circle pulled

by strings fast to
a hanging weight

when shuttled by the
playful hand

and i thought
what the hell
are they ever the right age
if that's what we're
supposed to worry about
so i bought it

MEDITATIONS

for miguel grinberg / 3 may 1975

why should i be embarrassed
sharing my dishwashing
my grocery sorting
when you have come
from sharing his meditations

it is not so different
it is precisely how
his verses and mine
have lain cheek by cheek

the lesson of
the juggler of our lady
is constantly before me

i pick up the mail
after dropping the garbage
and you read my poems

share with me
i am a domestic poet
tomorrow i will pick up the toys
do the laundry
write a poem of the tits of the mother
who dances before me

WEDDING HAIKU

wind blows
         shakes island
holed up they warm each other
and winter passes

VINE DELORIA MEETS A PALESKIN

it's not the chasm
it's the bridge
i'm afraid of

that's why
i believe in trolls

FOR THOSE, THERE

that wide space
which is maine

that narrow space
the brain

that space
beyond space
the poem

they are
brought together

we are brought together

even far away
the poems ring

i hear them
they call me
to that wide space

FOR TOM BLACKBURN

metaphor is all
and all
when come to
metaphor

"to bear over"

the one act
which makes us
conscious also
brave deceitful
and the like

subjective self

writers have three
thousand years of
history so must
start by baring self
then move to
things bearing on our
selves and make those
things and self
more in the world

we never knew we
did it and can not
even comprehend that
doing yet keep on

it is a lesson to
bear over and over

words for things
for words for things
and still have them things
and still have selves
and have the world

FOR LOUIS ZUKOFSKY 1904–1978

when you tell the truth
they scream at you

when you lie
they scream also

when you write poems
they ignore you

when you don't write poems
it's like being dead

     when you die
     nobody tells us
               again
     we are left to survive

     but we have what you have written
     and the words sing to us
     while we grieve that you are gone
     and that we paid too little attention

FOR THE O-YANKS 27 august 1979

this green square
tilted on end
is perfect geometry
in which the figures
move us with them
in their motion

there is no time
in this space
                    it is
a dance which need
not end
                we dance with it
a capella solo
eyes never at rest
taking it all in
the stretch of arms
sharp kick of leg
quick uncoiling
in response
                quicker
yet response to that
in this defined
and timeless space

THE WAY WE WERE

for jonathan williams / his fiftieth / 1979

that he used a lot of tabasco sauce
on one plate of scrambled eggs

that he looked like llud of the light
standing in at the plate

that he had the first hi-fi i'd ever seen
and fiddled with its controls
as if he were conducting it

that he played the first mahler i'd ever heard
the first bartok the first varese the first everything

that his books were so neatly arranged
but not by title or author or even subject
but by principles of design he learned in chicago

that when we were young we moved in the same world
and we lusted and loved together but not for each other
                                                    we said
and we told each other the objects of our desire

that he was the first one ever to put his belief
in my words into words on a page to be sold

that he appeared and disappeared and appeared again
and has always come and gone in my life
while i have sat still in one place

that he has come into that place and pulled me out
and taken me to meet poets i dreamed of

that williams and zukofsky and blackburn were mine
because he brought me to them

that what we have talked about for almost thirty years
is music art baseball poetry and life

that we have drunk bourbon, wine, beer, homebrew,
                                    shine, and club soda together
in rooms, honky-tonks, parks, and executive suites

that he has lived his life and i have lived mine
and it took a gap of ten years to accept each other's

that he has been a friend for three-fifths of my life
and he has held a manuscript three-fifths of that

that he has one year and eighteen days on me
and that is enough to qualify him as older and wiser

that he brought culture to me
and made me eat it

that we are friends
and we will sit down together at the table
that is prepared for us wherever and whenever that is
                                                    to be
and that at that table we will be greeted by the company
                                        of those who can talk
vidal, li po, bobo, dizzy, and all

and we will eat and drink and laugh and talk our asses
                                                        off
and play baseball and poems together

and have, in that place, all those objects of our desire
and once again we will tell each other about those
giggling like schoolboys up late at night
and finding the big world around us

FOR WILLIE SUTTON   2 november 1980

willie you went
where the money was
and began at
the age of nine

the report says
you robbed society
of two million
but i didn't know
we were the banks

of course it's easy
to speak of
glorifying thieves
but you did give
forty-three years
of public service
even did the laundry
at attica state
while nixon was
running for office

and you put on
costumes to
do your work
while the others
just put us on

and besides
like you said
the insurance
will cover this
and the rest
of our lives
has no such
insurance but only
bad actors
not knowing
the time they owe

A VILLAGE POEM

in the summer of '73
i'd had twenty years
in this place
                    my own
history

          a history
of places, things,
a piling up said one
a night-mare we
are trying to escape
said another

i sat in the white horse
with my son, nineteen,
beside me
                    the last time
we sat together in a bar
he was five, and the bar
was the cedar tavern
and a man gave him
and his brother each
a dollar for a toy

what history had done
to the white horse was
to turn it too small
misshapen dingy dark
ceiling too close

not even memories

me only forty-three

i started to be cynical
i started to be sorry
i had brought him
i started to apologize

but i caught a look
in his eyes and i saw
he saw the ghosts
saw he saw dylan in
one corner, behan
in another, saw he saw
all writers everywhere
saw those drinking
their lives away
still writing their
words saw the white horse
was bright and real
for him
          i shut up

and i remembered
my own history then
remembered the walks
twenty years ago
edna st vincent millay's
house or maxwell bodenheim
seen on the street
cummings in the back
of the eighth street
jackson pollock tackling
the eiffel tower in front
of the albert hotel
and all the bright moments

it's today for someone
else right now walking
in here young and eyes open
seeing the brightness

it's never, not
this particular way
for someone not here

it doesn't matter if
the crooked streets
the little houses and stores
or history or art
keep bringing them here

listen, some want to work
and will do so, even

      franz kline sat in the cedar tavern new hat on head
                                bought at cavanaugh's
      he always dressed beautiful
                          pollock walked in talked
                                drank got angry
      grabbed that hat threw it on floor jumped on it threw it

      ledge on top of the bar too far to reach
                        franz bought a round
                                  a week later
      pollock appeared again bought round sat talked stood up
                              pirouetted said
      look at my new raincoat just got at brooks brothers
                              franz said it is
      beautiful
                  jackson bought more drinks sat drank got mad
                              jumped up ran
      outside ripped off coat stomped it in gutter threw into
                            road under a cab
      and came in
            franz bought another round

50

it is history whether we
want it or not
it is what we learn from
it is where the paintings
come from and the poems

what? melville different, or
dreiser, poe, well yes maybe
james different but not
even that different

all young people come to find
a place and themselves
and their history and
to make their history
and to make their connection
the whole long line
of crazy people working
at work finding right places
where work is possible
where friends are possible
the whole long line yes
shakespeare had a place
villon peire vidal ovid
even homer singing
in some bar then

not that to drink
is to create or that
to be crazy either
not that to have friends
who do is to create
not even that to have
a place is to create
and certainly not that
this place is the only place

but that this place exists
and it might as well be
and we keep coming here
and using it for that

it is our place where we are
and it is the place where
the work gets done
as even tonight it gets done
and tomorrow when we are alone

because we have this place
and we believe in it

and it is still bright
and perfectly formed
and it is where we are

New Spaces

"seeing them i still open
still enclose myself in them"

TIME OUT

with even one day's worth
poems
          surrounded with these things
to find out what to care about

time time 'uncommitted free'

meanwhile sitting among all these things
all the time but only now to
notice and find out which

with only sons i see young
girls sprouting breasts while other
fathers see beards everywhere
darkening the chins of boys

meanwhile the papers are there to read
even when one doesn't have time

this is how one learns of the rebirth
of the everglades after fire and
how okefenokee is dying for lack
lack of that same fire
                    the swamp
does not dry out
               the dam built
to save timber outside the swamp
keeps the water too high

the swamp will not burn the natural
process of death and rebirth—are
you listening?—can not take place
the swamp is dying

                        across the world
the egyptians curse the rooshians
for building the aswan dam they
wanted

           everyone forgot about
the silting

           the silt builds up
in the dam itself it no longer
flows with the spring flood to
make the land rich by the river

they forgot the silting in plans
for the dam damned engineers what
do they know or care of history
which is neither progress nor new

instead the growing land disappears
sucked into the current not
relaid year after year after year

now the banks crumble in
pull of the water as magnet

something else is new too
now the nile doesn't flow into
the mediterranean

                  sea in the land
it seeps instead so the salt
creeps up that mouth that delta
that wellspring fouled

and the whole purpose of the dam
was to make power to make fertilizer

—camel shit!—to make the inland
deserts bloom
            and it does not make enough
to offset the loss from the banks
where there is no silt to come to rest

ebb and flood of the nile how many eons
we have disrupted destroyed

saying we even though they because
the only time we've ever refused
all for the wrong reasons of course
money and politics and ideology
and so the rooshians take the rap

we have forgotten how to be fathers
ought yes ought to watch breasts and
beards bloom we made them no? and
are entitled but further it is
our duty to notice it will keep
us from breaking the natural laws

we might hear occasionally these voices
and might have occasionally an idea
but the notion that we ought to be consulted
seems not to have occurred to anyone
not even ourselves although it ought to have

the notion that we might have ideas
and ought in any event to be consulted

every time myself this flooding
pouring out as if it were something

i'd forgotten it all in the damming
of the days and nights and never looking

more to have this—time time—and
the looking and to sit and he sd be uncommitted
so that the silt deposits and things grow

THE OLDER MAN THINKING OF KORE

the song rises

the skin shiny
and smooth

the belly free
at last

i am ready—

hi-yo!

she approaches!

FOOTPRINTS OF MAN-LIKE CREATURES FOUND

stopping to look
off to the left
hearing something
there
      "it gives a very
human aspect"

fifty-seven footprints
twenty are eight and a half
inches long
         twenty-seven
are seven point three

they figure to
four feet tall
and four feet eight inches

two people
walking along
singing a song
three and a half
million years ago

"by itself the ash
would not have retained
clear prints but it
appears it had been
wetted by a rain shower

and was slowly hardening
like plaster when
they walked over it"

walking along
singing a song
side by side

LESSONS I

the war was over
                    they found helen in
deiphobus' house

              he had taken her
there after paris was killed
                              against her
will

      she had given herself to paris
willingly enough

                  deiphobus was
not what she had bargained for

                              so they burst
into the house
                  both menelaus and
odysseus
          to kill these two

                              but as
graves tell us
              "some say helen herself plunged
a dagger into deiphobus' back"

this and the sight of her naked breasts so
weakened menelaus in his resolve
that "she must die!" he threw away his sword
and led her in safety back to the ships

LESSONS II

the point isn't
that he fought that war
or vowed that she must die

it isn't even that
they left together
spent the exile in egypt
went home to sparta
together

       it is that
moment
        and the dreams
that led him to it

the dreams
when someone
leaves us for
another
      and when
she is beautiful
in our eyes and
the other's and
the world's eyes too

so he raised his kinsmen
and their armies
and he fought

to kill her
and avenge his honor

the sight of
her naked breasts
ended this war

all through that war
he must have had
this certain dream
every little once in a while

this dream in which
he finds himself
again and again

he is bringing gifts
—beware a greek
bringing gifts—
yet bringing gifts
to her
          to ask
forgiveness
                since
we do decide we are
the one who's wrong

we ask forgiveness
in those dreams
while wide awake
we know how
wronged we are

in those dreams
we beg acceptance
and a smile

oh yes we know
that we have wronged

why else be alone

so alone we hope
to be forgiven
having done that wrong

in this certain dream
helen sits waiting

we open the gift
for her
          it
astounds her
and she smiles
then laughs

we too smile and laugh
as she accepts it
thus accepting us

so good in the dream
we wake sick with anger
having dreamed it

real anger that
somewhere deep
we still suck around
still beg

          even
menelaus begs
for helen's
naked breasts her
smile and all

even when we know
the loss and time
gone
     know that
it's over
       dead

we want it that way
and we would not
change it
       still
we want love just
as it used to be

we want buttermilk
breasts that perfect
face that acceptance

the tender love
she had once felt
for us we thought

even knowing all this time
she deserves her paris
and he her
       perfect for
each other
       just as we
had thought we were perfect
once

     even for the world
they are the perfect
couple coupled

yet we ask why
yet we dream why

yet we cry why
paris why him why
her
    where did i
go wrong

AFTER A POEM

i don't know if death
is an admiral in full dress

or a whore with skirt slit
up the sides of the thighs

or one of the queens

i don't know any more than
what does mother life look like

only that death and life
both exist and are

one is one or the other

the dancer is another story
and the fixed stare frozen
is another story also

they are the uniforms
i would like to know about
to recognize so I can
fall before or flee

ACTS

my son and i
walk out
in this cold october morning
toward his school

we hold hands

his other hand
holds a pennywhistle

he will use it
to accompany the guitar
in the morning singing circle

at each corner we cross
i am looking for you
while he and i walk and talk

i keep thinking
we will meet
at one of those corners
our paths intersecting
just as the clear note
of the pennywhistle
occasionally crosses
a particular chord
of the guitar
in the structure of some song

i keep thinking
in other words
that there must be a point
that we cross in common

and so this morning
we do meet
and walk together
half a block

he and i still
holding hands
you next to me
on the other side

one small moment
for you and me
to register our selves

and then later
after he is in school
and you are gone
i drink my morning coffee
and read the paper
again intersecting
this time with the world

i read that hugo zacchini
the first human cannonball
is dead

i read that all his life
he wanted to be a painter
and that after his retirement
he taught art to young kids

'yes, say for me'
he is quoted
'that my cannon
does me much honor
but do not
forget to add
that it is as a painter
that it is my ambition
to be known—
day be day
my cannon cannot give me
the thrills
that i can get
with my brush.'

lucky man who
day by day
first in malta
then throughout europe
then in the old garden

before me
- a little boy
holding my father's hand

went one hundred and fifty feet
reaching an arc of seventy-five

where was my father headed
what intersection
was i going toward then

a flash
a puff of smoke
a roar
and he would go
hurtling through the air

in an idea
he conceived
serving with the artillery
in world war one

so i hurtle toward you
and toward this poem
aiming for some corner
of our lives
where we can meet
this morning

i do not know
whether or not
there is a net
it never occurs to me
to wonder about it

the flash smoke and roar
take the forms of
an alarm clock
and the radio
and a small child
needing his bottom wiped

oh this act also
will be carried on
by my son
just as his son
learned to enter
the mouth of the cannon

oh i also wanted
to do something else

oh i also learned my methods
in some previous wars

THE PROGRESSION

                all i know
                the body
                the poem

that strange land
the body
        maps abound
but i am lost there

        have known yours
        and yours
                and yours

            i forget them all
            not touching them

            having not once remembered
            hair
                not hair i lived with
            ten years
                    then eleven

            not hair i see repeated
            on my sons
                    not hair i find
            on collar or in bed

        if you remember her hair
        she is already an object to you

neither object nor person
or i would remember
                    something

not even my own body
remembered
                    save in touch

I

toe knee chest nut
is how i wash this body

          two days a week i saw a man
          to tell my dreams to

                              that
          was so many years ago

          what i remember is i was
          always forcing myself into
          the cellar of my being
          because instead i wanted
          to ride always upward

     toe knee chest nut
     the game and song go

          i had to learn to go down
          in those dreams, into cellars
          of my being
                    instead of upward
          into head and brain and
          intellect which ordered action

still cannot bathe
from top down
as others do
they tell me

skin crawls at thought
of washing groin after
face
        foot after
groin after face

i don't know why

II

                phalanges = line of soldiers
                tarsus = broad flat surface
                metatarsus = at the back + tarsus
                cuneiform = wedge-shaped
                navicular = boat-shaped
                cuboid = cube-shaped
                talus = one of a set of dice
                calcaneus = heelbone

all wrapped in muscle
pulled and held by
tendons
        sinews that
we walk by

covered with meat
with flesh
        with body
that we talk of

the foot supports us
as we walk away our lives
'men who spend their lives
walking and talking' is
the way he put it

wash every bone
with care
                the
cloth poised

the water runs

III

suspending part of her weight
from the bar above
the japanese lady
much smaller than us anyhow
and small still since lady
walks her toes up and down
the back
            it is the final stage
of the massage and they are
fingers on the back

                are like fingers indeed
                with much the same construction
                some names are different since
                they have evolved to different uses

a lady sat
right next to the flea circus
in the freak museum
beneath the penny arcade

her arms were folded
visible under her satin blouse

anything for a hype

it's a living isn't it

with her feet for hands
toes for her fingers
she wrote her name
lefty and then righty too

sold postcards for a nickel
signed both ways

      again and again i went back
      to watch her
               wondered
      what kind of discipline
      could teach your toes to write
      when you still had your fingers

      what could drive you to it

they are like fingers
and the bones almost the same

IV

itchy feet
are not the same
as itchy palms

i don't like to walk

travel doesn't interest me

but i've been cursed
with itchy feet

if the body
contracts what it
deserves or wants
what are my feet
telling me itching
while i sit

contracted athlete's foot
at six while neither
athlete nor in
want of travel

have ridden with it
forty years or more

have often ripped
my toes apart
with painful scratching

have often winced
and shuddered in
the five and ten
when young when
faced with awful
posters of some
torn-up skin between
some model's toes

they always hung
just behind
the soda fountain

yet at night again
rubbed and rubbed
on bedposts and on
frame
          with fingers
and with nails and
with the other foot

relief from painful itching
was often promised

there is no relief
from painful itching
save the scratch

V

          this little piggy went to market
          this little piggy stayed home
          this little piggy had roast beef
          this little piggy had none
          and this little piggy cried wee wee wee all the way home

it is how we learned to count
so that roast beef has always
been a special food for me

and so that i always thought
it had to do with that
last pee to take for bed

and so that i always wondered
about the rhyme
                    how home
and none could match

the subtle pressures
of the culture

as the toes themselves
press against the
ground to hold us up

VI

one night
desperate
           cold and
stormy inside
she berated me
i did not know
how to make love

i felt her breasts
i rubbed her clitoris
i fondled soft her ass
perhaps then i
nibbled on her ear

oh the scornful look
oh the refusal

oh it's not enough
it's not enough

what of the ribcage
     though i knew one friend loved that
what of the arching back
     though i knew one friend loved that
the calves
     another

the knees
        another

all parts of the body someone said
'not erogenous'
                who said that

it was two in the morning
and the fight went on
until finally one by one
i kissed her toes
sucked them each
into my mouth
licked under in
the soft and hidden
parts
        rubbed against
the arch

she came then startled
and against her will
sitting in her chair

after this one night
she resisted my advances

she had learned that
her toes were erogenous

or my tongue was

and she'd thought
she had me beaten

VII

my own toes grow old
and no one will caress them

all that itching and rubbing
and walking and talking
and badly fitting shoes
have scarred them

now the nails grow strangely
curving round the ball
of toe
      impossible to cut

the nails are thick and hard

now i love them
because they are my own

we love only what
is our own
         or is
perfect in our eyes
in others

      there
is no middle ground

    i want someone beautiful
    and melting as has
    happened now and then

i will not settle

only those who move
in order to stop moving
settle

others
cover up the ashes
and move on

VIII

my first lover used her feet
as well as head and opened
up my pants by toes alone

that also was erotic
to a young man's sense

'ah, we were all beautiful
once,' is what she said
as she cut the roses

i had grown enough not
to be astonished that
she could use her toes
so well though she
still had her fingers

IX

this little pig
went to market
five sons times
ten toes is what
it comes to

        not
counting my own

the feet we walk by
as we walk by
as we keep
touching ground

as we keep moving

FOR HAN YU AFTER ALMOST 1200 YEARS

"people say
when your teeth go
it's certain
the end's near"
he wrote

he wrote
"but seems to me
life has its limits
you die when you die
either with
or without teeth"

he wrote
"this is a poem
i chanted and wrote
to startle my children"

all the while
i was reading him
an unfinished draft
lay on my desk

"the breasts
of the young woman
from st louis
dance before him
and their nipples

rise to his hand
and also
her legs
stretch out
trembling"

i wrote
"he is
twenty years older
than the young woman
from st louis

"he was
raised in yonkers
and now
he is
almost toothless"

oh han yu
we don't change

not people like us

we're impossible
the women
keep telling us

we're incorrigible

we'll do anything

THE DREAM

for r.b.

diana goddess
moon sister mistress
once

     still haunting
dreams though it
is fifteen years

you have changed
and now hermaphrodite
you are testing me
as if the testing
then were not enough

i thought i had either
passed or failed that
time gone by
         as if
you were saying i
had not been tried
at all that time

see your phallos lifts
a two-bodied snake
joined at the center
of your body

a double phallos
to be taken somehow
all together by me
or as two apart

your breasts are
still full as i
remembered them
with the nipples
even larger
                yes
we do remember

your sex is hidden
from me and i
remember that that
way
        though it was
always open to me
it was hidden all
the time as is the
way with all your
sisters always

now it is truly
hidden
            in the dream
i could not get
to it
        though i tried

in the dream i
am working even
harder than before
to satisfy

you were
never satisfied
although i always
thought you were

you did not tell me
that you weren't
until the very end

what you said then
was that i brought you
closer than any person
had
	you said that only
dreams had satisfied
you ever

		so now
in this dream
my attention keeps
shifting so as
to satisfy you

breasts cunt double
phallos all before
me and i shift tensely
one to another seeking

it was hard enough
before when i thought
everything satisfied
and found that nothing
did and because i
learned that lesson
i start sure that
nothing now will

i have left the
dream goddess i
am talking about
a real past
           a
history of
golden writhings
on your body
by my own

a body
i had seen as
heavy lead before
now something
new
        transmuted
base to fine
learning its
capacities as
never seen before

but in this dream
i am suddenly aware
my ass is being
licked through all
of this, all
my difficulties
finding you
              it is
a man
       it is a
man i know

it is not a young
man or some similar
scenario

                    it is
a man almost my
own age who licks me

like a satyr he is
tonguing out my
ass
        i tremble to it
as i tremble also
while i lick your
calm breasts and
nipples and the
double phallos and
your hidden sex

the satyr is intent
upon my rear
                    nothing
stops him
            let him be
my real friend as
in life but i
will not have it

in my dream i
object even as i
tremble to it

i cannot accept
his tongue or love

but i am intent
myself upon your
double phallos
as well as
your womanly
parts

but in the
dream you are a
woman and he is man

i build a case within
the dream saying in
my head this means
i too am now complete
or almost anyhow
                    i
too begin to become
all
     i too begin
becoming one and whole

i make the argument
with myself within
the dream
              afraid
of loving my own sex
for what that means

afraid because i like
what he is doing

but perhaps the
argument is true
and it is not simple
fear
       then i am complete

if i can give and
take it all then
i will be freed
from your anima
i lusted for

i will be free to
love our mother as
i want to
          with all
my dreams and self

with all my poems and
words

          with this dream
then i will be
free
      my self

SCHIZOPHRENIA

i go out
to buy
a garbage can
hand beaters
a steam iron
a stew pot
a double boiler
scissors
and then
a new suit
and wellington boots

i am making
a new life

in between
i stop
to call you

you are angry
and i don't know why

the anger spews
from the earpiece

i call you again
after the boots
and the suit

it has eased a little
but you are still
very angry

i go on
about my new life

i have promised it
to myself
whether or not
you are part of it

in fact i think
you are scared
of this new life
and being part of it
and that is why
you are angry

it will be weeks
until you admit this
but now i do not know
and can only guess

there is another day
when you send
someone else to do
errands i know
you should do
and which i depended on
for an excuse
to see you and
to face that anger
if it could come out
face to face

by sending that
other person
you have made it clear
how little there is
you can say

oh well
i dust my
wellingtons
and make them shine
day by day

and i continue
to plan
how and when
i might run into you

A BEGINNING

we are here
in this place

we hunt these
new beasts

we take their
hides and their furs
to the island
to meet the ships

we were brought
to do this
              in this
new place where
fog covers all
too often

the sun tells us
how the year moves

when the sun rose
in the notch
the priest prepared
for its coming
it was the new year

now it is darker
it is four months later
we watch the sun
dying slowly now

it will die
faster and faster
and the dark will come

we will be alone
in this new place
without the ships
for the winter

building our piles
of furs and hides

we were brought here
for this
          the mother
came with us
her belly filled
by the father

.   .   .   .   .   .

there are others here
with different faces

i have taken one
of their women
and they have taken me

we show each other
what we do

they know
these strange beasts
but i know the mother
and the father
and the coming
of the new year
and they
do not

her skin is a
different color
and the paint
on her face is
different too
and her hair springs
alive under my hand
and is black

i gave myself
to her
          my friend
gave himself back
to the mother

that has never
happened before

he asked the men
on the ships
to take him home
from this fog

they would not

i asked him
to take my woman's

sister
       he could not

he gave himself
back to the mother

he could not eat
the strange things
that grow here

and the bear
of this place
was different
to him
       he was afraid

i saw that this bear
was our bear's brother
and i welcomed him
as he welcomed me

and i eat
the strange things
that my woman
knows how to cook

  ·   ·   ·   ·   ·   ·

ah, even the rocks
are different here

still we can build
places to pray

and the mother of mothers
mother of heroes

the father of fathers
who is the sun
of the new year
all have travelled
here with us
in the ships
over the water

and the priests
have come
with the prayers

and we make
our homes here
and there will be
small ones too

to grow big
in this place

where we meet the
ships with our cargo

THE MAN OBSERVED

THROUGH THE KITCHEN WINDOW

I

BEGINNING THE PORTRAIT

it is monday morning.
he is washing
the breakfast dishes.
this is the easy day:
soft-boiled eggs, so
there's no frying pan
to be washed, and the
egg-cups and spoons
are easy once you remember
to run them through
hot water right after
eating. all that's left
are knives from the
jelly and cream cheese
and glasses from juice.
it is an easy day.
sometimes the children
drink out of paper cups
which should make it easier
but in fact they never
finish the juice which means
that the cups must be
carried to the sink, emptied,

then carried halfway back
to be thrown in the garbage.

          as usual, the realist painter
          watches all this through his own
          kitchen window. sometimes
          abstractedly he considers
          making thumbnail sketches.
          someday there will be a painting.

this particular monday
is clear and warm. that
is better. perhaps today
he will get some work done.
there are, after all, letters
which must be answered.
mondays that are cold and gray
hold everything up all week.

even better, this monday
he has no erotic thoughts,
no fantasies or dreams
to consider and disturb him.
his motor is off, he is
only slightly angry, and
the world has not yet
fucked him up. so he
finishes the dishes,
rinses the sink, forgets
to wipe the table, and
curses when he remembers.
the world has started.
he wipes the table,
trying to catch all the crumbs.
half fall on the floor.
he ignores them and goes

to the children's room
where he takes the pot
from its seat, carries
it to the sink and empties
and rinses it and brings
it back. now he is ready
to work. his own bowels
stir slightly. he leaves
the kitchen again, the
frame of the window now empty
save for the dishes drying
and the usual impedimenta.

the realist painter stops watching
and turns his own head inward
framing the scene in his head
the window, the dishes, the impedimenta,
the man discovered through the kitchen window.

II

THE CONCIERGE

occasionally he too looks
out the window while he
does the dishes. his eye
is caught, perhaps by a flash
of movement, or he hears
a noise. he turns his head
then and glances out and down.
he almost never looks straight
out across the courtyard
into a neighbor's kitchen
except by accident, since
he is not at all like his
friend the realist painter

who often spends long hours
watching, sometimes drawing,
sometimes just thinking.

he looks out only when something
attracts him, calls him to it.
sometimes it is a clutch
of women from the suburbs
come to visit culture
on a tour and he knows
their bus is parked, waiting,
in front of the building
though he cannot see it.
he sees a sculptor he knows
who's working as their guide
talking and gesturing. who
could know how to handle
these art-hungry women?
but the assignment pays
a little, and indeed the ladies
might just buy a painting
from one of the studios
they visit—or even
a contorted piece from
the guide himself! so
he does it for the money
one might say. why does
the poet do the dishes?

once, when he was still
married, he was in the
elevator, hauling his
laundry in a shopping cart
pushing the baby in
the stroller. a woman
from the building sneered

at him and made remarks
about his efforts. as the
elevator stopped to let
him off, he smiled and told her
he only did it to get his
wife to sleep with him.
the door closed slowly
but firmly the way that
elevator doors will do
and he kept the smile
all the way to his house.

nevertheless why is he
doing dishes? for the
money? does he know
he is posing for the
realist painter up there
in his window? he doesn't
even if quite often he
does feel he is posing
for something, someone,
when he stands patiently
alone at the sink.

sometimes it is the
children outside who lure
him till he turns to look.
not only his, but all
the children from the
building, fights beginning,
or loud and passionate
crying. his reaction is
immediate but not too
helpful, since all he does
is look. it is hard to
act sixteen feet above the

action, separated from it
by the window's glass.
and always he is brought
back anyway by the threat
of water overflowing.
besides, the window is
dirty, has not been washed
in six or seven years,
so that it is just not
satisfying looking through
it. he is not about to
swing himself out and
wash it, and the cost for
a professional is too
prohibitive. so the
window stays dirty, and
some sort of life
goes on outside it.
he does not think he
could spend his life
at a dirty window. he
is getting his chance
to find out at last.

RINSING HIS TEETH

after his lunch, eaten
at the sink, sitting on
the kitchen stepstool,
after salami on rye with
mustard, and chocolate
pudding left from last night's
dinner, after all the lunches
eaten on jobs he used to hold,
business lunches, lunches

eaten at the desk, ah he
thinks, today i will eat
a pear. the pears are gone.
they are not in the
big boy's lunch, he
packed that himself,
putting in an apple.
the little one asked
for one last night, but
he refused him. someone
has taken the last pear.
he crumples. it is
almost a pose.

        the realist painter in his perch
        by the window perks right up.

but he is not allowed
this luxury of paranoia.
the crumbs of rye bread
and the lingering taste
of the chocolate pudding
bring him back, remind him,
and he turns to the sink,
turns on the water, and
takes out his teeth to
wash them. full dentures,
they remind him of his age,
of all the whiskey he drank
losing teeth, of jokes
about clean old men, and,
subconsciously, perhaps,
of the defanged vagina.
patiently he rinses both
his teeth and his mouth.

the realist painter finds this
a funny subject for a quick sketch.

he wonders if he could pull
such a painting off.

he wonders who might be induced
to buy such an obscene painting.

MAKING THE HOLIDAY BREAKFAST

he is not alone this
new year's morning. he
makes breakfast in good
company. the three year
old sits on the stepstool
chattering, and eats toasted
raisin bread while the
breakfast gets made, and
brings the silver and
the jam and creamcheese
and the toast to the table.
while the boy is busy, he
busies himself with bacon
and with scrambled eggs.
he adds grated swiss and
parmesan to the eggs as
he beats them. he is piecing
together a year. now the
eight year old enters, to
help to stir the eggs.

he is not alone in the new
year, he is piecing it together.

he has put last night's
coffee on to heat, there
will be two cups worth.
and he gets out the cream
and sugar and his cup.

the realist painter is not yet
awake, his window stands empty.
no one looks out, looks in on
this splendid holiday breakfast.

at the party he was at
the night before he saw
a bed built in a bathroom.
he thought as he looked
at it how nice it was
that there existed someone
more hung-up than he, but
now, this morning, he is
not at all that sure.
every one of them at that
party had sat waiting,
waiting for gaiety and
merriment to start, waiting
for the party's start. they
had thought that this was
the beginning of a new time.
at one minute before midnight
he'd had to remind them
it was the new year coming.

the kisses were sterile,
on the cheek and brow.
there was no passion at all.
nobody danced. he had
dutifully sat and sipped

his club soda, had not
missed the booze, had even
thought that next year
it might be cigars that
he was fighting. was that
a resolution? he had no
way to know or not.
he had smoked one joint,
had gotten a minor buzz.
mostly it had just kept
him awake. somehow he
was piecing together
a new year, a new time.

      behind the empty window across the way
      the realist painter slept on. in his dream
      he watched people celebrating new year's.
      they had clusters of white balloons he broke.

coming home from the party,
awake and alert on the
grass, he wondered at the
mildness of the night, and
remembered suddenly a
new years twelve years earlier.
the wind had whipped at
forty miles an hour, the
temperature had dropped to
ten below, they had four
blocks to walk and almost
couldn't make it. he could
not remember what it was
that year turned out.

they all sit down to eat.
they are all quiet as they do.

the realist painter was still
not yet at his window, watching.
nevertheless, the year had begun.

bless the food we eat
at beginnings. we begin.

CITIES THIS CITY

the things they always complain of
coming from outside and again on leaving
there are so many of us crowded in here
and we are all so aloof and alone

we here are always alone
every city alone in this country
which has never learned to accept its cities
every city on its own alone and doomed
born to lose written on its walls

yet here we stay in it and keep coming to it
we keep pouring ourselves in and out

we light the skies with ourselves sometimes
sometime someone may be watching those lights

we are using ourselves people bodies
instead of trees and grass and earth
we eat people instead of eating the land
we watch love and hate bloom all around us
not weeds or flowers as in so many other places

we keep thinking we are making something
from our own bones and blood and flesh
and not like the others living off the land

we know that the oldest city was so
we know that the newest city will be so
it will always be the place the others use
while they keep complaining about it
while they send what they make from the earth
while they send what they can't use
while they send what they want to sell
for what we have to give them in return

they send their poets and their whores
their painters their conmen their dancers
their thieves their dreamers their murderers
and we add our own to these yes

maybe you cannot have one without the other
maybe indeed you need all in this city

i don't know if this is right
i only know the need to use one's self
to bet on one's self even when it's fixed
rather than watching things grow outside one
and then killing them and then piling them up

and when the ports and the crossroads
and the easy jumps across rivers
aren't needed any more for their commerce
the songs and the poems and the dancers
and the drawings of things imagined and real
which come out of the rub of people against people
will keep pouring out of the city's people
feeding the people who are angry feeding them

this feeding started in the first gathering
and will go on to the last gathering
because while the world builds itself in the void
people alone hunger for each other always

for whatever it is that only people can make
for whatever it is that only people can feed each other

THE HARDBOILED MYSTERY

dashiell hammett and maybe
raymond chandler too i am
reading you again after years
and yes i'd like to believe
the twists in the plots
came bubbling out almost in passing

i'd like to believe too
that you found those felicitous phrases
tripping off your tongue with no problems
but i know in all cases the lines
were sweated over to come perfect
or blurted out not knowing
what it was you were saying

then you were hung with it
had to follow it through
found yourself in positions
you didn't expect but had to defend
and you chandler popping those images
tell me straight weren't they simply evasions
didn't they just cover up the fact
that you didn't know where you were going
because i can see after the fact
that the plot line wasn't that carefully
laid down it didn't hang on index cards
neatly pasted on the wall before you
it got its own twists and twirls

until again there you were
waiting to find out what happened

oh my god how i'd like to believe
that living with a creative woman
dash was more for both of you
than hassling and moving in and out
and i'd like to believe also
that the drinking and the drying out
made sense as metaphors and
as a plot line too but i know
how hard it is living with any woman
or one's self and how you can
turn a corner and find the plot
gnarled up again and i know
how the phrases stumble and fall

i know where you come from
which makes me hope that heaven
is one long movie where it's all
straightened out so it will appeal
to everyone and everything gets settled
by the end and all the stars
know their lines and even the scenery is terrific

which is why this poem is for you
dashiell hammett and for you too
raymond chandler maybe and certainly
for me my own continental op
lost in this hardboiled mystery
in which nothing gets solved or comes clean

THE FOUR FATHERS

the first of whom
is clouded
                  is
not to be seen but
felt in the dark night
is *phallos* simply
is insertion, jet
feel him

later, so much later
feel his skin
                    smell
cigars or sweat

whatever

he is not there

he fills her
or does not

out of him is built

he is dark and inside

then the second appears
nourishing
                  he yells, shouts
he punishes and loves

he also takes the mother
but with deference
and is as frightened
sometimes as the child

the third father does
whatever the second did not
and does not do
whatever the second did

he tells secrets he has learned
and he creates his own mystery
since he is there for her
but also for himself

the fourth father is old
and we think him wise
and we find him a stranger
but we talk

oh i have been all
of the first three
and soon will be the fourth

each of the mothers
each of the children
know me differently

each has a different picture
folded in your heart

AROMAS

it stinks in
this bathroom
downstairs from
the organic restaurant
all fruits and vegetables
organic
   all meats
and poultry organic
and hormone free
and yet it stinks

and when the cats
shit in the clean box
that also stinks
while i make breakfast
for the boys and me

stinks stinks stinks
and as i turned down
to her she said
the plumbing broke i've
had no bath for three days
i stink
   she did

she was right
she stank
   the

acrid bite cut my nose
and i recoiled

she had not lied

so we coupled other ways
while that honest awful
stink hung on in mind

had she lied
                had
i not expected it
it would have hung
in nose as well

that night she bathed
and i went down

there was no smell but good
which itself was honest also

SUMMER SONGS

I

waiting for the afternoon
it comes
it is gone

II

fruit
flesh
in summer
all the same thing

i taste a cherry
i taste a plum
i taste you

juices flow

they taste fine
there's no difference

III

earth air fire and water
on the one hand

scissor rock and paper
on the other

earth puts out fire
fire burns up air
air dries water
water covers earth

whichever of us
was wrong
holds out our wrist

the other with
index and middle finger
together and extended
raps smartly

we are children
playing this game
but there are elements
of reality in it

IV

territory demands
we take each other's land
with knives
                mumblety-peg
calls only for dexterity
and elegance of form

we play one or the other
as the need moves us

territory is ruined
if one gives one's land away

mumblety-peg fails
when one doesn't care

V

there are differences:
in winter i shower
because i want love
or because i've had it

in summer i shower
all the time
              as if
plunging into the sea
had to do with
keeping my cool

VI

what i like
is seeing you naked

it is almost obligatory
in summer
              an impossible
favor in winter

suddenly i do not know
which to prefer
except that you are
more beautiful than
all the blackbirds
with their sheen-y feathers

124

VII

peaches plums cherries
grapes and berries

still lifes
on every table

i take
what i am able

CACTI

love comes
once a month
these days

i am not complaining

it drops on me
unexpectedly
just as rain does
on cactus
in nature
in the desert

it floods me
for a moment
forces new growth
drains away then
in sandy dirt

i am planted
in sandy dirt
insecurely

it is all
a conceit
of course

still
i am not complaining

126

i am stating
facts of my life
at this moment
and perhaps
from now on

i am
after all
still alive

i have survived
a long time

and i have watched
all the flowering plants
of my life
wither and die
because i did not
handle them
properly
or water them
as they needed
or perhaps
if the new thinking
is correct
did not know
how to talk to them

i am not complaining

i am learning now
that the cactuses
the succulents
even my crown of thorns
continue to grow
to survive

to flourish
without love
or water
more than once
every month

and it has taken
all this time
to learn this
and to learn
that they are my plants
as my life

yet it is true
the kangaroo vine
she left here
is still going

its tendrils reach
out to the lamp
down to the radiator
but this is an aberration
the exception
proving the rule

II

it is
opuntia rufida
the blind prickly pear
that first declared itself
as if in acknowledgment
of my own blindness

it refused to die
despite the fact

that i expected it to
and perhaps even
out of that expectation
encouraged it to

nevertheless
every time
i left this house
for any length of time
it sent out
new shoots
so that
when i returned
it had children
to greet me

they jutted out
and curved upward
at odd angles
and at odd junctures
from the main body

they were
bright green
even though
rufida itself
tends to blue
or gray green

now this cactus
will even grow
while i am home
and the shoots
continue to be
phallic in nature
just as i myself

have fathered
nothing but sons

cattle relish feeding
on the joints
of opuntia rufida
in the wild
and on its
small fleshy
bright red fruit
which i have never seen
but the plant
is supplied
with glochids
or thin barbed bristles
which fill the areoles
where spines would grow
in other cacti

these glochids
readily penetrate the eye
and blind the cattle
feeding there

next to rufida
there are two cacti
grafted together
as one

at the top
gymnocalycium
asterias
a bright orange globe
with tuberculate ribs

each tubercle swelling
just below the areole
so that the cactus
is called chinned

under it
cereus ocamponis
of which it is said
old stems turn
dull bluish-green
and the rib margins
become brown and horny

mine fits this description
it must be very old

the book also says
gymnocalycium
is self-sterile
in most species
and that hybrids abound
in this genus

next to that pot
on my table
a different variety
of cereus stands

it has just
been given to me
and i do not
understand it yet

it is tall
it is light green
it is shooting

a new growth
straight up
from its top

we watch each other
carefully
we will have to learn
to live with each other

behind this front rank
stand the others

to the left
echinocereus
a hedgehog cactus

it is self-contained
and silent too
as are all cacti
but has attracted
from somewhere
an unnamed succulent
which has sprung up
beside it

the succulent
is very young
but already tall
with small thick leaves

it is ready
for its own pot
but i am afraid
to transplant it

it is not
related to
the jade or
happiness tree
as they call it
in england
which grows
separate and distinct
in its own pot
a handspan away

this succulent
i am told
should have its
leaves wiped clean
every fortnight
but i do not believe
this happens
in nature

new york city
is not nature
and we do
the best we can
in its grime

since it and i
continue to flourish
i credit such happiness
as we have
to this jade
doing its best
in this house

i told you
i am not complaining

at the rear
of all these plants
rearing proudly
is euphorbia
my crown of thorns
which i rescued
from friends who
despaired of it
tired perhaps
of its stance
or its obduracy

having watched
the cacti grow well
i was emboldened
to try this one also
and brought it home
even though then
i did not know
its name

i was born
in east virginny
to caroline
where i did go
and there i spied
a fair young maiden
her name and age
i did not know
says the song

this plant
grows tall
with thin green leaves
small sharp thorns
and a woody curving stem

still it is
a succulent
i am told
and it has
a rare
hard
and terrifying beauty
that makes us equal
as we face each other

III

these plants
enlarge my landscape
and make it green

no this green
is not leafy
or flowering
it is not
the beauty
many depend on
but it does not
leave me
and it gives hope

spikes
spines
thorns
thin barbed bristles
protect it

and when you touch
we hold on

we do not
grab you

you must
come to us

like the rain
once a month
out of nowhere
out of blue
and beautiful
skies that rain
otherwise
on leafy
flowering plants

this is why
i am not complaining

i am learning
how to live

i am learning
i am neither rose
nor weed of the field
but did not know that
and suffered long
trying to be such
trying to grow that way

i am not complaining
i thrive
even though
i grow older

i grow stronger

the only ones
that i hurt
these days
are the ones
who do not understand
and try to
grab me
or come to eat
too ravenously
and are blinded for it
or those
who laugh
to see my
brown and horny
rib margins
my colors of
blue or gray green
and cannot accept
that this
is beauty also
and a way
to keep living
in a hostile
climate
in a soil
that would not
support an ordinary beauty

those who cannot accept
another way
to live

HOUSES

eighteen years ago
i left your house

it was your house

yes i brought home
the money
         we
did it that way
in those days

now again
i am showering
in your house
         "her bath, which she takes
         because he wills it so . . . .
         in his tub. in his water. wife."
         was even more years ago

             i do remember
             and i don't

getting undressed
i saw a silk robe
hanging behind the door

and the jars of oils
the soaps and powders

lining the shelves
beside the door

all in neat order
beautiful things

things beautiful
by themselves
and things beautiful
on your body

i thought how all
that i have loved
all that i have missed
is in this house

don't misunderstand me
i am not speaking
of romance
or rekindled love
or even second chances

nor is it a new obsession
with neatness
from one who's always
been the other way

if anything it might be
a lesson for younger lovers

perhaps even
for the ones
i come here
to see married

our first son
and his beloved

as if that action
by our child
allows you
to invite me
and me to accept
and that is why
i am in this house
far from my own

far from that house
i have learned
my own lessons in
in building

in any event
a lesson
here also

      in first love there are things
      we grow to as a habit
      and will never be happy
      without again
                  sexual appetites
      change
         it is easy
      to grow cramped and leave

      still i say again
      no matter what reason
      for the ending
                there are things
      we grow to as a habit
      without which
      we will not be happy

so it is
that years ago

i learned to love
your ways
so clean and neat

ways that cared
for beauty
and were beauty
and were
without
compulsion
          they happened
around me
without my knowing
and they were
caring ways

i've smiled at times
these eighteen years
realizing that
the only reason
i have folded up
my washcloth
in my bathroom
is because
you wanted it
that way
instead of crumpled
               while
all that is remembered
of our sex
are bits and pieces
of some short-lived scenes

no touches
no movements
underneath me

a few sighs
or groans
a few importunings
one to the other

a picture of your breast
or thigh or face or hand

but i remember
very well
the house
you gave me
and see it
here again

perhaps this is why
i am so pleased
that i have changed
to see it
through the eighteen years
for what it is
and what it was
for me
       not that
you have not changed
it's clear you have
it's clear we both have
but this part of you
has not
       and the part of me
that sees it has

.   .   .   .

now it is after the shower
and i have changed
in a much simpler sense

i am in some
new-found finery
a fop or dude
inside my western shirt
my shiny boots
and all the rest
as you have never seen me
and i feel i fit
in your house now
a stranger perhaps
because i am so proper
where as your lover
i stuck out
        it is
the proper way to visit
i am saying

but on your shelf
among the oils
and powders
is the frog
i bought you
our first christmas
twenty-five or more
years ago

i see it now

made of brass
a candleholder
on his back

        i knew
you wanted it
i saved the five
or seven dollars

that it cost
            i'm glad
to see it now
                it means
you really wanted it
it wasn't just a fancy

you kept it with you
and you use it now

there is a stub
of candle in it

perhaps some nights
you bathe yourself
by candlelight
                    i
see you that way

long baths as
i remember
                while
i lay in bed
reading
        or wrote
that first book

the one with poems
about you bathing

or just waited
in our bed for you

the waiting was not
always good
                it

destroyed the marriage
i have sometimes
thought
                  but not
the waiting
while you bathed

that was part
of what you gave me
as i lay in bed
and dreamed
                  a sense
of preparation and
of love and care

it was the other waiting
caused perhaps by what
i did to you or
what you thought i did

then after a while
i could wait no longer
and i went
                  you
were just as happy
and that pain
is gone now

i remember only
there was a woman
of rare beauty
                  a wife
who bathed herself
so slowly in my tub
that i wrote poems
about it

                in that first home
i ever had
                a home you gave
to me long years ago

        .   .   .   .

before the shower
i had taken a nap
in the guest room
of your house
                        i
dreamed of us
of course

we were naked
but only from our waists
on down
                as if to say
this is where we are
right now
                with the sex
outside and open

we were so afraid
in those days
and we didn't know it

in the dream
our tops were covered
our brains under cover
covered prettily
to face the world
and each other

perhaps that
might have worked
if we had known it then
to cover up our brains
and let our sex hang out

but we didn't know it
and we kept on talking

so i woke from that nap
this afternoon in your house
at peace with the dream
despite its sexual content
which aroused me
                    it was
not you so much as
talking to myself
the good doctors
tell us that

at peace i went into
the bathroom for my shower
where i found my past

and was at peace
with that too
as i am now in my house
writing this to you

the house i've fought
my way through to get to

this house which is
not so clean and neat
as yours
                    i am a man

i need a woman's touch
might be the pity of it
but i've learned to build
without it
        but now can see
how pleasant such things are
and where they come from
in me
      that is what
i did not know
          and what
i now do know
and will remember

Printed June 1985 in Santa Barbara & Ann Arbor
for the Black Sparrow Press by Graham Mackintosh
& Edwards Brothers Inc. Design by Barbara Martin.
The edition is published in paper wrappers; there
are 200 cloth trade copies; 150 hardcover copies
have been numbered & signed by the author; & 26
lettered copies with an original holograph poem
have been handbound in boards by Earle Gray &
are signed by Joel Oppenheimer.

Photo: Gerard Malanga

JOEL OPPENHEIMER was born in Yonkers, New York, in 1930, and was raised and educated in that industrial city north of the Bronx. He spent a year at Cornell University, a semester at the University of Chicago, and a year floundering, until he fetched up at Black Mountain College.

There he studied with M. C. Richards, Paul Goodman, and Charles Olson, and also worked as the school printer.

In 1966 he was chosen to head the new "Poetry Project" at St. Mark's Church-in-the-Bowery. He served as director for two years.

His columns appeared regularly in the *Village Voice* from 1969 until fall of 1984. He taught, and served as writer-in-residence, at City College of the City University of New York, until the spring of 1982, when he moved to New Hampshire and began teaching at New England College. On leave from that institution for 1984-85, he is currently serving as the Caroline Werner Gannett Distinguished Visiting Professor of the Humanities to the College of Liberal Arts at Rochester Institute of Technology.

He received a Caps grant in poetry (1970) and an NEA in poetry (1980).